Marisha Chamberlain

POWERS

POWERS

Marisha Chamberlain

Photography by David Goldes

Minnesota Voices Project #15

New Rivers Press 1983

Some of the poems in *Powers* have previously appeared in the following publications: *The Ardis Anthology of New American Poetry, Crazy Horse, Dacotah Territory, Great River Review, Madog, An Arts Journal* (Swansea, WALES), *Milkweed Chronicle, Prairie Schooner, Rapport, A Shout In The Street, Steelhead*, and *The United States in Literature* (a Scott-Foresman textbook). Our thanks to the editors of these publications for permission to reprint here.

The author would also gratefully like to acknowledge editorial help and encouragement from James Moore and Jill Breckenridge over the years these poems were written. Special thanks to Roger Blakely for his aid in the final editing of this book. Special thanks are also due to The MacDowell Colony, Peterborough, N.H., for the months of residence in which this book took shape; and for three grants that helped with the book's completion: a National Endowment for the Arts Fellowship in Creative Writing, a Bush Fellowship for Artists, and a Loft McKnight Fellowship.

Powers has been published with the aid of grant support from the Dayton Hudson Foundation, the Jerome Foundation, the Arts Development Fund of the United Arts Council, the Metropolitan Regional Arts Council (with funds appropriated by the Minnesota State Legislature), and the National Endowment for the Arts (with funds appropriated by the Congress of the United States).

New Rivers Press Books and the Minnesota Voices Project are distributed by

Small Press Distribution   and   Bookslinger
1784 Shattuck Ave.   213 E. 4th St.
Berkeley, CA 94709   St. Paul, MN 55101

Powers has been manufactured in the United States of America for New Rivers Press, Inc. (C.W. Truesdale, editor/publisher), 1602 Selby Ave., St. Paul, MN 55104 in a first edition of 1000 copies.

For My Sister, Nannette

POWERS

1. The Power of Light

State Fair

Alone or arm in arm or on another's
shoulders, through horticulture's honey-
comb, white cake sagging to shocked corn,
lurid blue tractor, harlequin quilt,
brute haunches of Percherons that hide
heads bowed to the stall's darkness,
stacked ducks, ratty hats, crockery gone
to smithereens in stifling tents, European
Legerdemain where Half Lady Half Baby
exhibits herself through striped fireworks,
Ferris wheel climbing the shattered sky—
How strange to be someone in particular.
A sledge hammer lifts. The crowd
wants to hear the bell.
You aren't the one who lifted the hammer,
yet your hands in your pockets tremble
with the weight,
and then you let go, and it rings!

Death of a Hen

My little brother and sister
chased a hen to death.
First, they were screaming with laughter.
Then they knelt down.
Mother looked once at their stricken faces,
picked up the twitching body,
carried her to the milkhouse
and cut her open.

Inside the red tunnel,
eggs were coming like planets.
The first one was big and almost hard,
the second and third eggs, smaller, smaller,
til the last, the seventh,
which was small as a thumbnail,
soft as a thumb pad,
and barely white.
Little pearl of feathered life,
little pearl.

Tying a Bell in My Hair

Morning darkness, by streetlight,
by the tree, the slippery elm
that sends new growth through scars
in the bark, I'm standing
with a man who belongs to someone
else. Trembling, my body
is a hollow full of bells.

I dreamed a woman tied a small,
round bell in her hair
above her eyes. When she moved, bending
her knees, her elbows, she rang,
rang, like a cat belled to warn
the birds. In the darkness
around us, they start to sing

and dawn, too long stifled
beneath the horizon,
advances its thousand bells,
its wind that makes the slippery
elm leaves ring, and the bell
I find in my hair, put there
by my master, the daylight.

The Birth Attendant

We stand all night to bring the baby in.
I'm in a lonely time and don't mind sleeplessness.
My sister and I stand. She's the doctor.
I leave an empty bed—I'm the helper, the ignorant
usher, the night watcher, capable at least
to hold the birthing mother's hand. I kiss it.
Allowed to greet a newborn, I'd gladly go
into fatigue that caves the brain like an old roof.
It's something like first love—birth. It takes over.

Wherever the unborn swell the ground or trees
or take up human bodies, I long to go
and draw them out, myself. Alongside my expert sister.
Water's in the childbed. Patience—dammed up water.
We move mechanically. The room stinks a little. Dust
puffs up over us. The birthing mother,
non-plussed by the disorder, begins a cranky weeping
and no one blames her. By dawn it hasn't come—
the shape we see cloaked in her belly that hardens,
then slackens.

I doze. Thoughts I left at home get up and stretch
and wander. Maybe a future lover steps into my rooms.
His footfall, unfamiliar, sounds nearer, then shies
farther. I don't care, I'm busy—I want to let him stray.
The newborn's father, leans his weight completely
on the wall behind the bed, rests a heavy hand
on the mother's shoulder.
She moves it off like an inert thing.
My unmet stranger brushes by again.
Like a ray of heat, I feel from him
a moment of impatience. I ought to know his name.

Lying in heart's twilight, the mother drops the sheet
to her complete nakedness, rolls on her side, pulls,
leans, ploughs into a weed field
of unknown length and breadth, unknown,
if she'll uncover, as she cuts the turf,
poison capsules, glassy specks, splitting atoms.
She heaves and drops her legs open.
My sister plunges in around the borning head as it shows,
then recedes, she slips her practiced fingers
between the twisted cord and the tiny neck,
pushes the cord to stretch around the shoulders—
all, still inside the mother. I squat by my sister,
hand her the stethoscope, then brace against her ache.

Our dozing flickers out. My dreamed-up lover
subsumes into the present—the baby comes—
not like a wanderer—she enters straightaway.
We stand up. We've stood ourselves to wakefulness
of a new order. A few minutes old,
I hold her on my knees, just cleaned
of the rubber shreds of caul, the violet cord
cut to a red stub, just washed of blood and cheese.
This small weight wants holding. I touch
from the translucent fingers to moth dust feet. Welcome.
Lonely or in love, I've never met anyone I wouldn't stay up
a night or three or twenty to see born—
if I could twist back time, I'd stay up for you.
But there's no need.
The unborn, every morning, pulse upward, underground.

Nazi Denmark: Jester to the King

This morning I went to the window
saw on the street the new badge:
a triangle, pink, as though snipped
from the clothing
to reveal a patch of skin:
the triangle over the left nipple,
white, pink, red in the chill,
tanning under the sun.

Your Majesty, the scissors—
the times are driving us
from our bright paradise
where I hid my sex in a costume
and slept at the foot of your bed.
Come, drive me out, through the streets
where you daily ride, where cheering crowds

are dimming in the light of war.
No hiding, no explaining
what we mean by these pink triangles.
The worst you'll hear
is what jesters hear: laughter
or terrible silence.

Under the Nazi occupation, King Christian of Denmark wore the Star of David to protect the
Danish Jews. At the same time, Hitler decreed that homosexuals wear pink triangles. The
king's response to this decree is not recorded.

Perennials

Clouds boil up over the mountains.
In a few hours, rain.
It's past spring, the fruit tree
is swathed in white, ripe in bloom.
I hold my breath looking on,
as though I could stay still
and the blossoms, never fall.

Last spring, I hung on the fence for hours
watching the white foal
work her wooden legs.
By August she moved in grace,
a foal no longer, a young horse
belonging more by the minute
until she escaped notice.

Wedding Clothes

I thrust, then tip the shovel handle
to open a crack so you can drop
the seed potato, lump with an eye
whose slow vision goes through particles
upward, to the light.
If we could see through the dense future
as the plant sees past shale, mud, grubs,
roots, moles in their burrows—
then we would know it was right to assume
the damp, white clothes of promising,
that these double, embryonic leaves
would rise to be green and dusty
in an everyday light.

Roses in Heavy Traffic

Sunday evening, no buses running, full
moon of the crimes of passion
and she walks home with an armload of roses
through the downtown, through heavy traffic,
teenagers, the perfume of exhaust,
by the alley, the shadows cast by headlight
on the siding of the funeral parlor,
black and white movie of roses: ruffled
knob of the blossom, wing of the leaf
in the woman's shadow arms, shadow
of sweater, long skirt, boot heels hurrying
with the soft burden, the small heads of newborns
thirsty for water on bending bodies.

A car slows down. A man slides his head
out the darkness of the window, pauses,
and vanishes in again. Three men leaning
on the board fence, turn their heads slowly,
watching her pass, but for once, say nothing,
because of the roses, fresh in the bud,
helpless crown of the other world
floating over the asphalt,
red sail that makes the bearer
the only ship on the teeming water.

Carnations at Midnight

Midnight, the phone rings, my sister is calling.
A carnation falls from the table. I pick up
the receiver, but leave the flower lying there.
Water won't do it any good. It was already
dead when I got it. A retarded woman fished it
from the garbage, said, *Here, gorgeous, this
is for you.*

My sister is in tears about my mother, who says
she can't come home at Christmas because Father
doesn't know about the baby. Mother won't say
what she thinks, she grows silent at the far end.
From the phone, she goes back to bed, lies
on her side with her back to Father

                                    who long ago
pinned carnations to our dresses the night of the
father-daughter dance. A steady fragrance blurred
the table where we sat—he didn't dance—my sister
and I waltzed each other, our faces flushed above
the flowers.

I grew carnations once. Only two small blooms from
the long row, just on the day the rows of beans
ripened. A carnation, blooming among vegetables,
the thin stem jointed like bamboo, the long green
cup that holds the burst of lace. My sister sighs.
Inside her belly, the baby opens the fingers
of its hand.

Corazon Amurao

I have uncommon sense:
I lie under the bed.
Through long daylight hours
I contract my body
to the comforting, hard wall
I press at thigh and knee,
at elbow, nose and forehead,
force myself to breathe
without raising my belly,
and then force my mind:

In case he can count bodies,
I unlearn numbers for him
then, for myself,
subtract what's familiar
from voices I hear scream,
then voice, itself,
from those loud sounds:
I turn them industrial,
the soundtrack of the city.
My name means *heart*,
my capacity is nothing
but to go on throbbing nonsense
within what's still alive.

Corazon Amurao: the only survivor of the murder of eight student nurses in Chicago, 1964.

20

Amaryllis

Frances paints the flower
whose name means shepherdess
or emperor: *Amaryllis*,
type: *Imperator*.
She says she must
subdue the orange,

release the light
into three wet trumpets
and in the mirror
she paints in the background,
three smaller horns,
echoes. The flowering

plant grows from its pot:
each bud opening
gives her three days
before she must move
to the next.
Yet sometimes she can't paint.
She knows it's anger,

but she slows into sleep
in the turpentine fumes,
lies down under the flower.
Anger used to be a bloom,
bright, and then, disappeared.
But her husband is really gone.

Clutching the stalk of a paintbrush,
she must rise through the shade
of Amaryllis
to command the orange,
to shepherd the light
onto the canvas.

21

2. Destructions

Powers

I should have placed
my five-year-old hands
on either side of your face
that had contracted
to a dark, raging mass, Father:
I'd seen Superman squeeze
coal into diamonds and
I should have pressed
til your face turned white
and lit up from inside.
I should have force-fed you
my brother's dinner
after your "compliments"
drove him from the table.
The food, growing cold, glowed.
I weighed fifty pounds.
Full-height, on tiptoe,
I came up to your thigh.
I could fit my fist
like a plum inside yours
and I should have made you
smile or died, trying.
I mean, murdered.
But I ignored you.
That's how I failed you,
why you stayed unhappy.

James Earl Ray

A boy who hides in a dump freezer
hides well, the freezer
won't open from the inside.
They'll find him years later:
mud, rags, old hair,
old white bones in the white box.
When James Earl Ray
went to the deep freeze,
somebody followed each step
in his shadow, somebody crowded
where he hid.

Tennessee June, too green,
too much sun, too much rain
on a pile of leaves.
Ray put a ladder on the prison wall,
ran. Now he lies under the leaves,
lies with his arms
around Martin Luther King.
How should he talk to the black man
who begins to die all over again,
fingering places bullets will enter.

The mountain man calls out
within the ring of troopers,
of dogs, straining on their leather,
calls softly:

James?

In 1974, James Earl Ray, convicted assassin of civil rights leader Martin Luther King, Jr.,
escaped briefly from a federal prison in the wilderness of East Tennessee.

The Housework of Night

When I got home
the birds were singing
though it was still dark.
I saw the tulips,
small jars of darkness
against a black window.
Getting ready for bed,
I found the surprising red
of menstruation,
the dark jar of the body
turned upside-down.

Like a minister's wife
who cleans before bed
so death can come in the night
without shame,
I rinse my things in the sink.
The hours have run through me
like water through a filter
and now, with dawn,
I wash and wash
the crust of wakefulness
from my face
til my head is light
and hollow
and hunger leaves me
as though for good,
as though death
has entered my house
and sits next to me in a rose shawl,
the sun coming up in the window,
and I revolve into sleep,
letting the flowers
of my life
fall:

the flowers that perfumed freely
and those tight buds that refused,
the sharp colored points,
the sloppy fans,
the cut stems, wilting
and those that took root in the water,
all trailing away from me now,
while death naps in my head
where the rooms are cleaned
to her liking.

We, Then Children

In your place, you've sent this sad uncle
after many years, tired, overweight, formal.
He wants to take me to a restaurant.
When I saw you last we were seventeen,
scorned bright lights, interior decor.
He reads the menu, avid as a hen.
In your father's car, dusk to midnight
we drove a road overarched with branches,
headlights off, the car top down, nighthawk
swooping in wild grape, elm and as night
invaded the province of upholstery
I felt you hard against me, and through
our clothes, my breasts under your
hands—your hands, familiar, false now
against the glare of the water glass.
You butter three rolls, stir
more sugar into coffee.
We, then children, happy to go hungry
and hesitant in any sacrament, paused,
turned home to our parents' houses.

The Stars Are Apple Clusters

Exhaustion builds a maze of branches
behind my eyes the first day
I pick apples. Day's end, my hands

still reach to pick. Like gloves
gone threadbare, gloves with holes
I put those hands away

in my pockets. Darkness unleashes stars
and I connect them in dark trees: the leaping
impulse of my hand toward the studded

branch. A dream smears me apple red
and apple green: I straddle a dozen
gleaming ladders, roll apples

into my mouth to collect in my half-bushel
stomach with the trap door chute
to a crate big as an empty city.

Night falls down on my head like a tarp.
I rip a hole in the night
and reach up to pick the stars.

Mona Lisa

1

The sun sets as I drive down from Red Wing.
I leave behind me, by dark,
the big lake, the sugarloaf,
the white rock where the Indian woman
leaped to her death in the water.
Maiden Rock. As I pass beneath it,
she plunges again into the river,
then out of a watery chrysallis,
her body gathered in a single curve:
the moon rising red behind a skin of cloud.
Swollen at the horizon,
now the moon condenses, whitens,
climbs the sky,
takes its place on top of the dark
below it like a black dress
and out of a black coif it shines,
the craters of the moon
through the gauze of distance:
the features of a face
and a smile.

2

I'm small and home sick.
Mother lays out for me the big black book,
Art Masterpieces, its cover so heavy
I must lift with two hands.
I move through the cave bulls, El Greco's storm,
the journey of the Magi with monkeys,
til I find my woman.
I see nothing remarkable in her smile:
I don't know yet this is the Mona Lisa
and not the mother of God. Her face, more godly
than the frightened Virgin, more certain
than Mary at the foot of the cross;

this unknown Italian woman
through da Vinci's hand gathered
all the lost in a curve
before she stood,
stepped away from the painter
into her perishing world.

Against *Three Sisters*

Once when I was twenty, and you, thirteen,
were warring with Father, you asked to borrow
my straw hair clasp to tie back your long hair.
Girl, he called you, tore it from you,
broke it on the floor.

We three sisters did stand as we were painted:
half-naked, in half-slip, garter and brassiere.
But we never trapped a boy in the bathroom with us,
never made you watch—you pounded at the door.
Borrower, grown brother, take all we have and wear

our underthings, our hairpins, our hours
at the glass. When Father trapped you,
wrenched you to the mirror,
we three sisters, long present in that air,
looked helplessly through you into our faces, our hair.

Three Sisters: a painting by Gregory Gillespie which depicts a tiny boy trapped in a room of half-dressed women.

End of the Season

Overnight freeze,
the apples
send their spirits
back through the twigs,
the branches,
the trunk of the tree.
They go limp
from inside out.

In the picking
crew's quarters,
the breakfast cook
is up and washing
in cold water.
By the pump, he squints
at the sun
on the apple trees,
the hanged fruit,
the end of the money.

Winter Washday

You collected snow every day of the week
and melted it in a barrel inside the door.
Through with the dark things, two days
on the washboard in that strong, lye water,
your fingers would all gather.
Sheets and the white things boiled on the stove
with soap shaved off with a sharp knife,
and you fished them out on a long stick,
holding them out from you, scalding hot,
sliding them into the rinse water.
They hung outside til they froze dry,
the long johns and overalls,
standing up stiff and laughable,
and you brought them inside and stood them
against the wall, the whole house
growing cold because of them,
until, all at once, they would clump down wet
like somebody falling out of bed,
and you strung them on the line that crossed the room.
In the dark, you stumbled between lines
of clothes, every night of the winter,
dreaming that you had to launder the snow,
gathering sheets of it into your tub
while more fell through the bleaching air
and your husband pushed you away in his sleep
from the handfuls of cloth you were scrubbing
over the ridge of his backbone.

Canary

Late fall, when I was seven
I saw a canary
in the barnyard, sudden
yellow on the weathered fence.
He let me come to him.
When I caught him,
he pecked my hand,
but he hopped eagerly
into the cage
where he lived longer
than he could in the cold.
He sang over our beds
and in the dark, flexed
his wings, he was a gold
heartbeat in a grey room.
He died soon, first shredding
the cuttlebone, scattering seed—

After months of estrangement,
I hear my lover's voice nearby
and try to call
this sudden longing, hatred,
when it is only song: brief, shrill,
a flutter, a nuisance
of feathers.

The Bed Is Empty

While you, the husband, make the bed, do the dishes,
your wife goes to work, your daughter gets the school bus
and miners on tv go belly-flat on conveyors into coal.

Coal coughs up a dozen dead at the cave-in, and water,
your dishwater, spits up the twenty-six from a Kentucky
flood who are now lowered on tv into the ground.

Your imagination lights up, giddy as the headlights
of cars in procession from the midday burial.
You stand on the doorstep as they pass, one eye watching,

the other eye, looking over your shoulder for the dark man
to hit you in the face with a spade. (Your heavy face,
your arms, thick and able; your body's forty solid years.)

Time passes as you think of it passing.
You see your wife and daughter laid out dead
while you stand at the foot of the bed, crying *Lazarus!*

but the bed is empty.

Oceanography

I stand inside her door.
She gets into the bath to avoid me.
I wait because of a photograph
of her in white stockings,
climbing down rocks toward water.
She's six years old in the picture,
her hair falls into her eyes
and the dress rides up her leg.

She steps out of the bath now,
seventeen and naked, except for mascara,
displays before me her fine, starved figure,
her shadowed eyes that dare me to note
she's drunk again before noon,
and so nearly still a child,
she flies at me naked, her fists
pounding my shoulder.

The drug counselor once asked her interests.
After a long pause, she answered,
Oceanography.
In that pause, I saw her again,
age six, standing at my elbow, my desk
in the light of the gooseneck lamp.
She'd crawl into the bed we shared
while I stayed up in my pool of light,
turning each time she spoke in her sleep
to answer her over my schoolbooks.

I crawl in now,
not to sleep, but to wake her.
Here in the cramped bed sisters share,
where her fists only gesture against my shoulder,
I heard her call me in her sleep,
a small voice speaking through an ocean.

3. Force Fields

Two Sisters in an Arbor

The striped quilt rises over her belly,
trails onto the grass.
Her second, unborn, makes the stripes ripple.
I sit nearby in a rocker, each stroke
of the runner carries me after her
deeper into the arbor.
Under the canopy of green,
the bunched fruit is black, full—
the skin splits, she grips my hand and bears down.
When we were girls, we stole the grapes.
Now we are forced to harvest.
From here to the far end of the arbor,
we follow the vines down.

April Fool

Somebody has the sense to bloom
Tender and rose
In the same huge night
Where trucks and elephants hurtle through
Somebody has the sense to kiss
Here in the month when the moon is full
Every night for us, April Fool.

We don't need sleep
The night's forever
You live with me in a cup of tea
Green, Chinese, and the watery air
Slows us down so we kiss again
You'll never need anything but my kisses
You'll never be hungry, April Fool.

Our mansion's in a lilac tree
The bee makes its buzzing circuit
Between us,
Brushing you, brushing me
I'm the liar. I say all this is new.
I've never loved anyone but you
April Fool.

Peeping Tom

He knows all the bedrooms,
the mess on my dresser,
the red flannel shirt on top of my hamper.
My poster of white flowers in a blue window
is one of the riches of his collection,
more so our bodies,
especially where the flesh
gathers in hills away from the bone.
The woman in apartment three reads in bed,
the sheet barely covering her breasts.
In another window, a man moves his wastebasket
next to his chair, clips his nails.
The girl with the red hair brings two cups of tea
into the bedroom where her boyfriend
is unzipping his jeans.
She pulls the shade, not exactly sure why,
nothing out there but a tangle of shrubs,
vines around elm trees, old logs, sticks,
a falling down wall,
lights and shadows falling from thirteen windows
that show tiny movies where nothing much happens.

Desire for Cold

In late afternoon of the year: late fall,
I abandon my peace with the sun, put on
the rough twilight jacket, push
the buttons through slits only by feel
in the dim light, make myself, not cozy, but
ready: dress like a soldier,
eager for the future.

Dawn had worn my thin, pink dress. Keep it!
I forswear spring when I dressed
carelessly, not quite naked, but always askew:
a strap always slipping off a shoulder.
I break faith with casual summer,
the need for shelter only at night
to block the stars that distract from sleep,
to keep the dew off.

As cold, at first invisible, puts trees
to the torch, then strips their leaves, as each day,
colder, brings clarity, each day, clearer and
death more active: not summer's lenient decay
but the bite in the air, everywhere—I stretch
my hand through the open door to feel the cold,
approaching night. Nothing clearer than cold
to fight and I need to fight.

Enormous Children

1

In early family pictures
the little ones are solemn,
loyal, barely standing
against their Daddy's leg,
and one's a babe in arms.
Years pass and one day
the babies are children
puffed up too big
for the dining room table
and with enormous gravity
that pulls all food toward them.
Their every whisper
is a major disruption.
It seems Daddy's taken
to standing on the table
to get their attention.

2

While Mom and Dad
sip their evening wine
in the low, white living room,
giant teenagers
return from play rehearsal
with three friends.
Politely bowing, introducing,
trying to be graceful,
they fill up half the room
even crowded together.
Don't get up, Mr. and Mrs.
Chamberlain, all we want
is a drink of water.
For the next three hours
the tap is constantly running,
Dad has an ear trained

to the pump in the basement.
In another while, two of them
stoop through the doorway,
proudly present the parents
with a nice bowl of popcorn.
Each popped kernel is the size
of a grapefruit and dripping
in butter. The bowl itself is
too big to fit
on the coffee table.
The parents ask
for it to be placed on the floor,
decline the gallon tumblers
of cherry limeade.
The guests go out the back
door at eleven,
ripping the porch off the
outside wall as they step out
under the stars,
never looking back and not
meaning any harm.

3

When the eldest is asked
on her first date,
the father calls the three
enormous daughters
down to his study
in the garage.
Towering over him,
they have to stoop and crawl
in the door, as if
it were a rabbit hutch.
They request to sit on the floor,
politely overlook
the size of the furniture.
He turns on the radio to his favorite
jazz station, setting the mood.
Pulling out his chair and being seated,
he chuckles, clears his throat:

I've always tried to be perfectly
open with my daughters.
Now, you're all pretty girls,
I mean that,
nothing wrong with that,
that's just wonderful.
The daughters shift their knees,
becoming still again when they
realize they are tearing
the carpet.
Only that the members of the
opposite sex, myself included—
he ends making vague and graceful
half-circles in the air.
The sisters hold their hands in a
refined and nonmuscular way, cupped
one in another in their huge laps.
Father straightens in his chair.
Daughters, really, I think
you know where I stand, I—uh—
guess this is a little silly.
The three nod quietly.
The floor trembles.
One allows the tiniest sigh,
the door blows open.
It's the eldest daughter,
who whispers in her softest voice,
DADDY, I'VE GOT TO GET READY
AND GO.

Halloween Dinner

The pumpkin is the first
to move from the food it was
to a solid ghost life.
Suddenly every food on the table
has a spirit with a carved face.
We want to stop this eating,
but the knives and forks
move over the feast
with a terrible life
of their own.

The Man in White

The man in white
outside the orchestra hall,
tough and gorgeous in thin, white cotton
on a chilly night,
standing behind his lady,
his hands on her shoulders, without lust
or desire of possession,
rather, as though he were steering her
through the dark.

Out in the pasture, beside the milk cow,
the bull lies down; huge, pearly-white Charolais,
the white hairs curling between his clipped horns,
his eyes closed under white lids,
and the sock of his balls
lying half on the ground
as though he were done with it,
like an oriole's nest through with seasons.
He's through with siring
and ready for the celestial sphere.

Adam and Eve

While the older children
were gone to school,
Rex and I played in the marsh.
Once we made a nest
in the cattails:
rush floor, high green walls
and nothing else but sky.

Rex wanted to kiss
but I put my hand
over my mouth
because his sister, Goldie,
had told us about Adam and Eve.
She said Adam and Eve got naked,
then put their bottoms together.

I couldn't speak to Rex
for three days.
At night I kept dreaming
he came through the window,
right through the glass,
and forced a kiss
on my sleeping mouth.

I woke ashamed of my dream,
washed my face
and ran outdoors again
to wander the garden of paradise.
The tree,
the tree that should have been
like any other tree

was now showing pink
at the bud.

Nakedness

1 The Hill

It's weather in which one can go
naked on the street,
a day a woman wears a lace camisole
under her workshirt, so she can unbutton it,
so, raising her arm to wave,
she can feel her navel blink into the light.
As she climbs the hill
the young man on the scaffolding
makes, not a wolf-whistle, but an elaborate
trill, scattering notes that praise the day
that now happens—oh, just happens
to include her.
And he will, only after she's passed, stop,
still whistling, catching his breath on a down-beat
and then continuing the melody, turn
to look at her:
her back retreating, the shock of bright hair
above the blunt collar of a shirt like his own.
Between her shoulders, hidden from him,
the wind is touching her belly, her ribs,
through lace eyelets.

2 Home

Allowed to do anything
behind a lace curtain, a pulled shade,
a locked door, why must we quarrel?
We stood together in the brewery garden
and watched peacocks drag their tails
through the dirt like expensive dresses
used wantonly by women who know the first silk
is the naked skin.
The dirt in the walkway behind us was the past,
the peony bush in the distance, the future,
and we were nothing but conscious of light,
conscious of movement forward.
A peacock raised his tail as we passed,
pivoted toward us til we could see
the bright side, the thumbprinted fan
and I thought of watching you take off your clothes.
But we don't live in a garden
and because a bed is sometimes confining
we forget that we make love along a journey.

3 Drawing

You ask if I will pose for you to draw me.
You've drawn me already, every time
I've held myself still for your touch.
When you are away, the lines dissolve,
my body goes into the dark within my clothes
and I forget myself
like a tramp standing at the side of the road
who will not travel nor lie down,
who twists the wool tighter, even in the heat:
a man becoming his clothes, for whom
undressing will soon have no meaning.
Why am I drawn like a daughter to his sorrow?
My body proves my parents once were lovers.
I slipped naked from their state of hope,
though now Mother and Father are so far separate,
imagining them together is an insult
as though I had forced them to take each other
for my sake, against their will.
In Mother's attic is a bundle of love letters,
words, though she may burn them, that cannot
be unsaid: set down here he praised
her skin, here, ellipses in which he touched her,
her fierce response, here in salutation.
Draw me, then, on paper, against all foreboding,
and I, to bribe the future, draw you here:
ankles, long legs, your fine head, the line
of your elbow, shoulder, your hipbone, your genitals
at rest in a calm light.

4. Prayer

Beauty

A woman at a party asks my height from across the room,
notes my sculptural presence. In my stammering
the room grows quiet and a man I desire
who speaks only to her, turns to me for a moment.
By the time he turns back, I've seen through his eyes
she is more beautiful than I and far more

careless. Part of my burden is desire,
its awkward measure when I am alone
and count out the times he looked my way
against the trips to the Frigidaire.
I dreamed I woke up ugly, chinless, alone, a presence
only to myself, and thought I was rid of desire.

But then, three children came to my door, too young
to notice my ugliness, who cared only that I be kind.
I wanted to be merely kind and ugly, but so help me,
I loved them with a love that had to be careless,
            it was so unbidden.
They had come to see me. I stepped into the light
to be beheld in a body no longer mine.

Moon in the Millpond

Naturally, it's full moon
when the birth begins.
Your labor starts and stops
and we, your attendants,
wait, giddy and useless
as drunk wedding guests
who, in the ancient story,
went running out-of-doors
to where the moon lay, drowned.

As the story goes,
we weep and throw nets,
disturb the image in the pond
and come up with nothing.
We try to hide our scatteredness
here in your room,
while you frown, remote
below the surface of your labor.

As we sit by the bed,
we sober and by morning
have learned the indifference
of grasses that border
the pond. We brush your hair,
feed you ice, shush you
when you ask if the baby's real
or only wishful, and

she in her own time
breaks into air.

After the Polish Lesson

After my first lesson,
you ask me to say I love you in Polish.
I give you what I remember:
the word for book, *ksiazka*,
kredka, the word for crayon,
czerwony, for the color red.
Lying in your arms, in the dark
I want these words to describe us:
a scribble of heat, red, on a page
of the New World.
The phrase you want does exist
in the ancient language
and I could rise, turn on the lights,
cross the house to find it
but at this hour the other knowledge
holds me. Children of wayward
immigrants, we sigh and moan,
our breath unbroken into speech.

Napoleon as a Flood

for J.

Napoleon should have had feathers
and you, red plumes, a crest
of black and iridescent patches
for wings, so you could rise
in natural flight, unconscious
of striving.

You stretch your hand on a scribbled
map: Napoleon's route through Europe.
Messy as history, you mutter.
Napoleon was sung out of exile
to the border. Songs not wonderfully
made, he said, but excellent
in feeling.

You feel within yourself the strength
to march across oceans to Paris.
Mornings, you rise to your work, burning
at the lack of greatness in your era.
If you had wings!

Cries—*Hail!*—by the river.
Strange cries after his name:
*Long Live Death! Napoleon! Down
With Human Enterprise! Strangle
The Babies In Their Cradles!* Napoleon called out
alone within his empire:
All I see is rabble.
All I hear is frenzy.

At least for an hour he should have been
a trumpet vine to draw birds
to his flowers. On St. Helena
in his small rooms in the narrow
house of his final exile, he recalled
five days he fought
without taking off his boots,
without eating.

His companions at table nodded, slept.
He went out in the fog and refused
to come in. His battle was against his bed,
not to become cotton stuffing.
You work yourself to exhaustion
as though by work you could gain such weight
as to lay your body in the scales
alone, opposite the world.

He inspected his stored clothing:
the uniform he wore as consul,
the cloak of Marengo, in silence.
He climbed back down the closet
stair, stepped a wide circle
around his bed, brought his companions
into his chamber, stood them,
marked their heights on the wall.
Then marked his own height.

He should have been a flash flood,
able to rise on whim,
leaving behind his new order
in the brilliant pattern of debris—
and you, a flying fish at the crest:
your very body a colored shimmer,
diving ignorant into fresh light,
into the physical future.

Princess Kay of the Milky Way

You stand on a straw bale
in the horse building,
braiding little ribbons
through the mane of your best filly.
She blinks, dips her chin.
She likes to be groomed
and you whisper to her for hours.
Yet all along her neck
are the hairs pulled tight,
the small, nervous signature
of beauty.

In a booth across the street,
photo buttons, two-fifty:
Creative, Corrective Posing.
Creative, Corrective Lighting.
When you get to the head of the line,
the photographer lifts your chin
with his finger,
adjusts the lights.
Your newly pierced ears
burn and sparkle.

If your working clothes
could be blue chiffon!
But already, the real Princess Kay
waits in the wings of the bandshell
for her coronation.
You sit in the back row,
picking at your sweatshirt,
jealous and relaxed
as she steps out in those
satin shoes, those heels.
She lifts her hand to the crowd.
A parade begins behind her.

Loving in Winter

When the first snow falls,
she is eating tiny white flowers.
Her mouth is cold,
her tongue is a piece
of supple ice.
She wants the water from her mouth
to take a new form:
as heavy snow, it'll slow down the man
who's travelling through.

Let Me Hold the Baby

I want to hold the baby
whose hands slap and
poke, and close around
a hank of hair
softly as a crescent wrench,
who keeps its parents
up night after night,
the bald monarch curled
on its father's shoulder,
quiet as long as he'll
walk it up and down,
who makes across the lawn
in the morning,
like a sidewinder after
the world's great treasure,
a croquet ball,
and the baby I dreamed
I tied to a tree,
patient until morning,
a wet leaf stuck to its head,
and the newborn I dreamed
asleep in a bed with bars,
its cheek flattened
against the bedsheet
and a hand-lettered sign
on its crib:
My name is Charles.
Be careful what you say to me.
I don't talk yet
but I remember every word.

We stand together,
childless, in the mirror,
your beard, coarse as straw,
the lines in my face:
the inventions of time
to distract us from the days

when we went everywhere
in someone's arms.
Sometimes we try
to carry each other,
even now. We never get far.
I want to hold a baby.
Let me hold the baby,
even when it cries: cries
and is still held,
and cries and is held
without rocking or
pleading, cries
and is held,
is held, is held—
I want to be the large
and patient one,
and I want to be the one
with the tear-streaked face
within the cradle of arms.

Still Life for My Brother

Here's the toad you carved me out of coal,
concentrated darkness pointed toward the window,
beside a rose drifting in a glass.

The water within the curved glass wall
captures and inverts, like a shrinking lens,
the scene outside the window: sky becomes a lake

that emanates light, the chimneys,
pilings for a missing dock,
lawns and gardens thatch the buildings: it's Europe.

Remember the night in downtown St. Paul
we walked below trees strung with tiny lights,
camouflage, you said, for filthy big business?

I argued for the lights, that if we were in Paris
you would find them lovely, and somehow you agreed.
The light of a hundred tiny bulbs, as you spoke,

showed me the faces of your regret,
worlds you gave up to organize the miners.
Yet I admire your single light,

your simple demeanor in public, in private.
I've lost your easy connection with strangers,
but I know you—and when I take the rose's part

and drift through little Europe, I can't
bring you with me, yet often feel you near
as though framed in the same window, you hunch

below me, dark-eyed, guarding the plain version
of the world.

The Young Dancer

The young dancer
wants to be
The Sugarplum Fairy,
but that is ten
years off. This year
she is a Toy.
When you are a Toy,
you want to be
a Cousin. The Cousins
wear flounced dresses,
tight coats, they
dance in pairs.
At least, she's not
a Rat. They never
get their steps right.
They have to manage
those sticks.
When others go to dinner,
they have to practice
again. One prefers
to be a Toy, a Cousin,
even a Soldier,
though they sweat
terribly in those
red uniforms.
Still, it's better
to be a Rat, than merely
to practice.

Willa Cather's Final Trip to Nebraska

I've buried them in the country graveyard.
I always thought I'd die out here
and not end up to be anyone
but a two-line obit in a farm paper.
I fear it now, against all evidence:
my books, the apartment in Manhattan.
And now they've left me all alone.
But it's the order of things
that the mother and father die first
and the daughter close up the house.
Still, when I stand on the back step,
the country is overwhelming
and Mother's not here to call me silly.
I've found an old photograph of myself
as a baby. I'm sitting in Mother's lap,
her hand lies on her black dress
beside my cheek and her other hand
is holding me, hidden in my baptismal gown
which is moving in the picture, swirling,
and my mouth is open as if to speak.
I look at peace with my surroundings.
I'll admit it's a little blurred,
but I'd like to live in that photograph:
to be a face, human, about to speak,
yet unconscious of itself:
a face dissolving into its surroundings.

5. The Will to Live

Horse and Rider

The little girl's horse
ran his leg to the bone
on barbed wire.
Now the girl and her mother
follow as the horsewoman
leads him across ten acres
and into the trailer.
Under the vet's needle
the horse struggles
while mother and daughter cry
and the horsewoman holds the horse
who fights against what coaxes him
through the loss of blood,
tugging the hull
of the ship of hair
toward the deep water
of the ground.
He gallops to the surface,
then sinks against the one
who struggles to hold the head
in her arms.
See how they ride!
The small horse,
the huge rider.

The Pregnant Woman and Her Sister, Asleep in the Same Bed

1 The Pregnant Woman's Dream

The baby was a melon
of flesh, smooth
all around. When I got
tired of the weight,
I could scoop it off
and set it on the kitchen
counter, blocking it
with a soup can
to keep it from rolling.
One day I grew tired
of being pregnant, altogether.
I wrapped it in a towel
and locked it
in the empty strongbox
which I lifted to the back
of the closet shelf.

2 The Sister's Dream

I went to the closet
and opened up the strong-
box, where I'd locked
the thought of a baby
away. Inside the ancient
towel, nothing
but a small, black
tooth.
I planted it
in a pot of warm mud
and lay down again.
As I slept, a bush
sprang up.
Its leaves were
the faces of my nieces
and nephews.

The Window

The children's hospital window
looks out on wild cucumber vines, grape-like
in leaf and tendril coil, but spreading
through spikes of burrs.
And on the window sill a blue plush dog
looks down on the girl
as she sinks on her white raft—

If the doctor won't
cry, don't
look at him,

or Mother, either, who turns her face
from how he sends the girl
straight through the window
where she will climb the vined hill
with her savage blue dog
and when Mother calls,
will brush off the voice like a burr
stuck to her pajamas.

As If Hands

—*As if hands, undoing our clothes
from the inside . . .*
                                Tom Lux

I step from solitude to you,
not naked, but the quartet
in my chest, fumbling
with strings, winds, valves,
buttons in cotton.

As if from sleep, I present
myself in a torn night-
gown, buttons undone,
the crowd bursting to you
through music, flannel.

New Words for the Funeral Mass of Pamela Mason

1

In the name of our fathers, slouching at windows,
waiting for us to come home;
and of our brothers, grown large, silent,
embarrassed with us, their little sisters;
in the name of our uncles
who look us up and down, curious—
in the twilight of the family,
still heated by old desires,
the small flower of the protection of children
wilts inside the large, hot bodies as night falls.

And without invoking the names of our mothers,
who, in the face of certain fears,
became merely larger versions of ourselves;
rather, in our own names,
in the name of Maura and Kathleen, of Marisha,
Gail and Candy,
and in the name of the girl who died,
whom we bury now, Pamela,
in the name of her body and ghost divided,
from the body we let Pamela go.

2

Late November's short afternoons,
I sat on the porch folding newspapers
as dusk came on,
slipping the raw edge into the fold.
She was missing, her picture printed
on every front page:
sleepy eyes, broadly spaced,
freckles, cleft chin and light hair,
reddish, shining—was she only hiding
away a little while?
Forty times that afternoon
she disappeared out of my hands.

3

Her death day passed
without a stir. The long, blue car
stopped by the roadside.
No one saw the private struggle
or felt her fall. A stranger
stopped me on the route
to ask the time.
I was struck dumb.
He hurried on, silent, angry.
At dinner, a hush fell on the table.
Mother said, *An angel*
just sat down.
It was an angel in stained clothes,
a blue-faced angel. My sisters
cleared the table,
we scraped the tiny bones,
washed the plates, while
the angel crept past
our slouching brother
into our room
and walked across our beds.
We'd follow to find Jesus
sleeping on that trail.
We didn't pray hard enough
so he got tired
and the murderer got ahead of him.
When Jesus woke up,
he was angry.

4

Morning, we schoolgirls
on St. Francis playground
gathered in a knot on the ice
to repeat eyewitness news:
Body of Pamela Mason, Lamb of God
found in a snowbank, who takest
away, in a cornfield,
the sins of the world,
seven miles south of town.
Have mercy on us, slashed chest,

slashed face and hands,
bruised arms and neck, and molested.
Gail and I go
to visit church, before recess
is over, pausing in the dark foyer
to knot the red scarves
at our throats.
We hurry past the windows
of the virgin martyrs,
straight to the altar of Mother Mary,
who enfolds us, together with the infant,
Mother, in whose blue lap we are buried,
resting our foreheads on the cool brass rail:

Hail Holy Queen,
Mother of Mercy, our life,
our sweetness and our hope.
To Thee do we cry, poor banished children of Eve.

Behind us, light moves
through the body of Agnes,
outlined in glass.
St. Agnes, with her burden of flowers,
like an armload of wood.
Beside her, the window
of Maria Goretti, dressed
also in white,
likewise killed at the age of twelve,
stumbling from the temple
of her body, broken in,
blessing herself as she fell.

5
Out of the trough filled with snow,
the body of a girl rises,
is raised and stood upright again,
snow sifting down from the torn blouse
and the blood.
The murdered girls of New Hampshire
rise and travel in the winter dark.

They are so eager to speak
through the channel he opened
in their throats.
Was I really stabbed or did I pass
through the eye of the knife?
They muse about it,
who share common marks of a certain
village to which they return
with scars that are the most relaxed
zones of the body—
scars with rays that shine inward
til the body of nothing
is entirely fearless,
full of courage,
taking up no room.

MARISHA CHAMBERLAIN

daughter of an artist and an itinerant college professor, grew up in Colorado, Texas, and New Hampshire. Since attending Macalester College, she has made her home in St. Paul, Minnesota. She holds an MFA degree in creative writing from Goddard College. She writes plays, stories, and essays, as well as poems. She serves as Literary Consultant to the Cricket Theater in Minneapolis, where she is also Playwright-in-Residence. *Powers* is her first published book.

THE MINNESOTA VOICES PROJECT

1981

\# 1 Deborah Keenan, HOUSEHOLD WOUNDS (poems), $3.00

\# 2 John Minczeski, THE RECONSTRUCTION OF LIGHT (poems), $3.00

The First Annual Competition

\# 3 John Solensten, THE HERON DANCER (stories), $5.00

\# 4 Madelon Sprengnether Gohlke, THE NORMAL HEART (poems), $3.00

\# 5 Ruth Roston, I LIVE IN THE WATCHMAKERS' TOWN (poems), $3.00

\# 6 Laurie Taylor, CHANGING THE PAST (poems), $3.00

1982

\# 7 Alvaro Cardona-Hine, WHEN I WAS A FATHER (a poetic memoir), $4.00

The Second Annual Competition

\# 8 Richard Broderick, NIGHT SALE (stories), $5.00

\# 9 Katherine Carlson, CASUALTIES (stories), $5.00

\#10 Sharon Chmielarz, DIFFERENT ARRANGEMENTS (poems), $3.00

\#11 Yvette Nelson, WE'LL COME WHEN IT RAINS (poems), $3.00

1983

\#12 Madelon Sprengnether, RIVERS, STORIES, HOUSES, DREAMS (familiar essays), $4.00

\#13 Wendy Parrish, BLENHEIM PALACE (poems), $3.00

The Third Annual Competition

#14 Perry Glasser, SUSPICIOUS ORIGINS (short stories), $6.00

#15 Marisha Chamberlain, POWERS (poems), $3.50

#16 Michael Moos, MORNING WINDOWS (poems), $3.50

#17 Mark Vinz, THE WEIRD KID (prose poems), $3.50

#18 Neal Bowers, THE GOLF BALL DIVER (poems), $3.50

Copies of any or all of these books may be purchased directly from the publisher by filling out the coupon below and mailing it, together with a check for the correct amount and $1.00 per order for postage and handling, to:

New Rivers Press
1602 Selby Ave.
St. Paul, MN 55104

_____

Please send me the following books: _____

_____

_____

_____

_____

_____

I am enclosing $ _____ (which includes $1.00 for postage and handling)
Please send these books as soon as possible to:

NAME _____

ADDRESS _____

CITY & STATE _____

ZIP _____